MY DARLING CAMEL

By the same author

Saying Hello at the Station

MY DARLING CAMEL
Selima Hill

Chatto & Windus LONDON

Published in 1988 by
Chatto & Windus Ltd
30 Bedford Square
London WC1B 3RP

British Library Cataloguing in Publication Data

Hill, Selima
My darling camel.
I. Title
821'.914   PR6058.144/

ISBN 0 7011 3286 8

Photoset by Rowland Phototypesetting Ltd
Bury St Edmunds, Suffolk
Printed in Great Britain by
Redwood Burn Ltd
Trowbridge, Wilts

Contents

ACKNOWLEDGEMENTS

Acknowledgements are due to the editors and publishers of the following magazines and books in which some of the poems appeared:

A3 (Oxford University Poetry Society): 'The Small-Mammal House'; BBC Radio, 'Poetry Now': 'Jacko's Girl'; *Encounter*: 'Looking for Camels'; *Gown* (Belfast): 'The Hyacinth Man'; *The Green Book*: 'Bid for the Summit' and 'Early Nights'; *Honest Ulsterman*: 'The Sea-Water Hall'; *London Magazine*: 'Eating Chocolates in the Dark', 'The Last Flight of the Friendship 27' and 'The Assumption'; *London Review of Books*: 'Mother Stone' and 'Not all the Women of England'; *The New British Poetry* (Grafton): 'Looking for Camels'; *P.E.N.*: 'The Unsuccessful Wedding-Night'; *Phoenix* (Australia): 'Diving at Midnight' and 'The Ptarmigan Hunter'; *Poetry Book Society Supplement*: 'The Holiday-Makers' Daughter', 'Saying Goodbye to the Suzuki Man' and 'Ouarzazate'; *Poetry Review*: 'A Ski-ing Accident'; *The Times Literary Supplement*: 'Lotty'; *Transformation – The Poetry of Spiritual Consciousness* (Rivelin Grapheme Press): 'The Darling of the Bathing-Pool Attendant'.

The author would also like to thank Hilde Gauthier-Pilters and Anne Innis Dagg for an excerpt from their book, 'The Camel' (see p. 54).

Diving at Midnight

She's been diving at midnight
with Harry again,
and this morning she has realised,
with a kind of helpless joy
that changes everything,
that she was born to be a diver:
every day until she dies,
she wants to stand,
with nothing but her Speedo on,
and stretch into the dive
like a high note; fly beautifully;
and enter the deep water like a die
on which your life depends.

She turns her chair into the sun,
and takes her T-shirt off,
to feel the sun shine on her breasts.
It touches her like sleepy babies
when your milk comes in.
It isn't true, she thinks to herself —
letting her mind wander
to the Arctic night,
and a lonely hooded waterfowler singing
to the sky —
it isn't true
that suffering in empty solitudes
is all man has to bring him close to God,

as poor old Igjugarjuk seems to think,
creeping along Prince Albert Sound,
steadying himself
on a bone harpoon.
He carries a beaded quiver and a bow.
He's stalking seventeen large geese.
He's listening

for the creaks and groans
of ice collapsing.
Carved goggles made of driftwood
curved by steam
protect his cold eyes
from the polar light

that whitens roots
and bones and stiffened hair
and kisses blown
against the wind-blown snow.
His people drift
among the shadows of the glaciers
and comb the hollowed plains
for wolverine and owls.
They're slow. They have to be.
They live curled up,
like the blue-glass beads
on the quiver that chink
against the bow-shaft bone.

The Sea-Water Hall

i.m. Eileen Berryman

The illuminated
DO NOT TAP THE GLASS
flickers in the darkness.
All down the hall,
fish circle sadly
in their twilight cubes.
The amphibians have little beaches too.

Here's a nice spot –
a perfect naked man,
three inches tall,

is sitting by a rock-pool.
He's writing something in a book.
When the keeper
drops a pinch of powder
from the sky, there's a lady
who runs up with a picnic plate
and catches as much as she can.
Come on, John, she says,
you really ought to eat something.

They seem to be trying
to kiss – in air
that's too viscous for them.
He climbes onto a ledge of rock
and stares at the painted ocean.

She fingers her neglected curls
and looks across at him
as if she'll never kiss him now.
He's coughing phlegm.
It slithers down the inside of the glass.

The gang-connector's not working properly.
It's getting hot in there.
He dives into the water
like a knife,
disturbing the forests
of green eel-grass.
The lady covers her body
with cream, and wishes
she were happier.

If you do tap the side,
she won't look up.
It's triple-glazed.
She can only hear
the keeper's dry fingers
and the bubbles rising.

The Holiday-Makers' Daughter

It doesn't matter what she looks like.
She's in one of her moods again,
and her parents, God bless them,
have driven off in their old Ford,
leaving her alone
on a rock overlooking the sea,
with the key to the bungalow,
in case it starts to rain,
and something to eat
in the fridge.
It doesn't matter, her mother had said,
but her father was red as a beetroot.

She will uncurl in her new-found solitude
like paper flowers from Japan
that grow when you put them in water.
She will develop
a kind of passionate detachment,
like a hen. (At night she reads
The Elegant Sayings Of The Lamas –
'a hen when at rest produceth
much fruit', that sort of thing.
She tries not to see the hen
too literally, but to get a feeling
of purity and earnest calm.)

Father Biddy, The Horse-Guard Priest –
who was he, she wonders,
with his shaven head and long black skirts
and his grey that he galloped at dawn?
She did know one priest, Father John.
He visited the Pet Cemetery
when she was doing the flowers,
but he was fat, and holding his hand
was like holding a helping of trifle.

He hid pennies in his habit
and asked the girls to find them.
She couldn't learn peace of mind from him . . .

I need a father, she concludes,
who would find it perfectly natural
to roll my body into a ball
and leave me in peace in a sandy cave
like the mummy of Uan Muhuggiag . . .
She's just nodding off on her warm rock,
a neat furry bundle
smelling of aniseed and myrrh –
not 'unfurling' at all,
or feeling 'nice to live with' –
when she hears the Ford
backing into the lane,

and picks up her binoculars
as if she's watching the birds.

The Hyacinth Man

All afternoon eleven men
lift silver weights
above their heads,
and feel their bodies
tremble like water,
or fish that follow currents
in their sleep,
and the gym walls thicken
like the sea-bed.
And when the tall proprietor
comes to the door
with his keys,
the athletes move like sails

to the light, blinking
as they loop blue towels
that smell of palm-oil
round their necks
with big loose hands.

And in the lonely castle
on the hill, the painter-king
is kneeling at his easel
spitting milk.
He is blocking his ears
to the screams
of small sunburnt women
stabbing each other
with stiletto heels.
The points of his moustaches
twitch like dirty dogs.
Why is he pulling
the baby hyacinths up?
To see if they've got roots!
the great man says. Come, come,
he's irritated
on his sick-bed
by his own last desires;

let the gentle nurse
turn out the light,
and usher in black dreams
of athletes from the gym
approaching lovers'
polished arms
like bulls,
whose grooms hang flowers
round their necks.
The gym is closed.
The castle on the hill
is lost in sleep.

Only the nurse is still awake,
her yellow apron
and the old man's shawl
padding
her wooden chair
like fat.

The Significance of Significance

She was worried he couldn't be happy
just loafing about by the river,
like she liked doing.
Plans, and plans about plans, and sex,
was *his* idea of happiness.
He wore a floppy hat.
She felt so lonely!

Another thing, she couldn't spell.
Laborinth. Itiniry. Elann.
She cooked him cockles
in a thick orange sauce,
and bought him a suit-case –
'for the Great Man'.

They sat on a rocky mountain
dressed in leather.
Sardines and beer.
Parois vertigineuses.

Their children were his books.
She understood that.
O Significado De Significado,
lecture notes.

'The blissfully well-run nursing-home'
is now public knowledge –
her little lump, like longing,

13

prized from her oesophagus;
her crawling from the hut
on her knees.

A tortoise-shell comb,
embroidery,
The Crack.
A lovely moth.
'The nurse is a crashing bore'
. . . poking about among her mysteries.
God bless you, Patty.

The Darling of the Bathing-Pool Attendant

Little feathers
journey past my cheeks
like boats.
I'm bubbling diamonds.
I'm just a head.

It's not a place
where people say hello.
They sunbathe
on their coats
without the sun.
Their favourite food
is sunflower seeds
and violet turnips
that they grow
on dung.
I call them nutters.

Can you see the silver ring
that swims along beside me
like a pet sardine?

I tell you something:
It means love.
(Men slide them on your finger.)
Land is still.
(If they get wet, they scream.)

The bathing-pool attendant,
who's amphibious, and kind,
says BEAUTIFUL THINGS HAPPEN
WHEN YOU SMILE. Such as?

This blue aquatic life
I'm leading: SMILE,
like a seraph paddling
among coots; BELIEVE!

I believe in lying on the banks of pools
even when there is no sun.
I believe in crocodiles.
I believe in love.

Red Cross Man

He is the Red Cross man.
He never comforts me.

We eat a lot of sugar.
There's no blood.

The texture of his red moustaches
frightens me.

He's not normal.
I'm not normal.

Everything is beautiful
without my son.

Queenio

Sand the risen peach, swollen with lust,
introduce a finger-nail tentatively
under its congested lip;
the juice will coil down her wrists
and lonely open hips, restless,
engorged with maggots. *Please come home.*

Lust has turned her hidden milk to bone.
Peach-blossoms stiffen,
goat-thick orchards sink,
eyed beetles wink and push like hounds
against her skin; *peach-girl, don't go.*
Shaky, untouchable, defiled by desire,

she casts around for somewhere soft to lie.
Come here. The knee-deep fruit play Queenie
with her loving soul, stripped clean
and tranquil by the coloured mouths
of peaches soft as eiderdowns.
They whisper *Queenio.* I said *Come here.*

Peggy

He loved the sunlight –
this was in New Mexico –
he loved the sunlight,
and he used to go for long walks
with the llama, Peggy;

and when his mother died,
one night in June,
he brought the llama with him
to the funeral:
standing like a queen in the mist,

batting her big eye-lashes
like cream.
His mother died
to get away from them!
She suffered terribly.

He used to be a tailor
like his father –
pricking his pot-belly with the pins
and sucking the red-currants
that he made . . .

His mother was a gold statuette . . .
He wanted so much love,
that was the trouble,
yet, if you tried to smile,
he looked away.

The llama called him
Chocolate Eyes.
She said, *Don't cry*.
She was the only thing
he wanted in the end.

Natural Wonders

i
The lovely boy
washes himself all over

in a ski-hut. His mother sends
a new suit every year.

'He only cares about
his mathematics.'

ii
He's tired.
He hates the snow.
He can't stop masturbating.

Each little death,
each floating point cries
Heaven, where are you now?

iii
The handsome mountain-dwelling monk lies dead.
Something is wrong with the electric fan.

His secret love-affair
exceeds his wildest dreams,

while here on earth
the other monks are lapsing.

Note: In the technical term 'decimal floating point', the sequence 2658 13, for example, would be used to represent the number 2.658×10^{13}, or 26580000000000.

Lotty

A white South African depressive
is kneeling on the veldt in Waterberg
training the beam of an electric torch
onto a little garden, where a king and queen
in white are watering their fungi-beds.
Baby soldiers wriggle on the paths,
and lift their heads from time to time
to suck the lovely globules forming
on the queen's black jaws . . .

He kneels by the nursery all night.
It's true he isn't well.
His wife died, and he lived alone
with Tame Toktokkie X and Tame Toktokkie Y.
His six-inch mother scorpion,
who carried sixteen babies on her back
in pairs, died recently as well.
He used to call her Lotty, or Carlotta,
his mother's and his grandmother's name.

Lucy

They lie down naked in the spider room
where legs are ears. They listen as they spin.

Then Lucy takes him for a walk. My dear,
in half an hour, she is in love with him.

Ulrike Meinhof, sing angelically;
Mongol invaders, bathe in padded light;

it is the Buddha passing on his elephant.
Lucy, take your love and follow him.

Benjamin

I am so close
I could kiss you, Benjamin.
(Our eyes never meet.)
Do you remember
slicing shins like fruit?

Do you remember
stepping through the snow
with nothing on?

(I'm pulling off your jeans.
I'm very close.)

You dance and hide
and live on peas
like necklaces.
(She wishes you would smile,
but you don't.)

You're sleeping on the floor
beside your *ra*
where crow-black songs
revolve, revolve, revolve.
(Your mummy thinks you are a sort of ghost.)

The Cupboard

He was a mother's boy.
He hated everything.
His lips were blue,
like cellophane, or iron.
He lived in a sort of cupboard
off his studio.
Even his mother was afraid of him.

No one approved of the marriage.
A fight broke out,
and the huge marquee
sank to its knees
like a horse.

Anxious women, swollen seas,
premature ejaculation every time.

She was an angel.
The pianist himself
was in love with her.

She wore bright yellow shoes
as if a field of buttercups
lay at her feet.

They lived alone
with an old she-goat,
painting pictures
no one could understand.
Sometimes the sea
came right into the garden.

They started to climb the steps,
holding the puppy.
'Ah, it's so peaceful here,' she said;
but when the dog died,
and he buried him,
she lay back on a deck-chair to calm down.

While they were eating
delicious home-made pasties,
she was thinking *I would rather be alone.*

At night he moved towards her
like a ship.
Nothing seemed true.
Her scarlet blood turned white.
She stretched out on her back
like sheets of ice that echo
when you touch them.
'I want to go to sleep and dream of B.'

The sun shines on a pair of woollen gloves.
A little dog appears above the snow.
His honey colours say, It's me she loves.

I'd better say goodbye before I go.

Plums

The music rises like a party dress.
Nocturnal marriages are always best.

Parrot feathers. Ancient seas. Soft plums.
Shelter in my bedroom when she comes.

Shirley Doesn't Live Here Anymore

Someone's little breasts
are sticking out.
The photographer
is beautiful.
I'm Shirley.

I'm not a man.
I'm kissing her.
She's dead.
I'm wearing an enormous coat.
I'm crying.

Proud Algol winks
and pumas doze.
Tut tut. Dead women
in white sheets
are going home.

We glide.
We climb.
We want a bar of chocolate.
komme komme komme
says the Lord.

Higher Things

Your mother was calling
for more and more Marigold gloves.
We went into town and bought buns
from a woman who knew you as a child,
then we sat below the lighthouse
talking about the Blessed Jan Ruysbroek
and coming to no conclusions.
In sitting, just sit.
Our buns were covered in sand.

You came to London
for my Wedding Day.
I was blinded by the sun,
then I saw you, and your hat,
and your preposterous Maori curls.
The ushers smelt of T.C.P.
We understood nothing but kisses,
and by the third day I was crying.

We were stuffing ourselves
with strawberries
on the top of the bank
while our babies slept
in the strawberry beds.
Didn't Sally have a birth-mark
on her neck,
and wasn't there a man
in swimming-trunks
who sang all afternoon
in a voice like Eddie Cochrane?

We decided to be
the first Polar women –
we mapped the Worst Journey
on my polyester sheet:

Edward Wilson
pulling the sledges
towards the Farthest South
with bandaged eyes.
He imagined the snow
swishing underfoot
to be the leaves
at Crippetts Wood
sighing for the love of God.
O keep on pulling towards the Pole,
LABOR IPSE VOLUPTAS
is carved in the terrible ice.

As we were eating doughnuts
in your house in the woods,
you squirted breast-milk
into Greta's tea. *He alone*
in Highest Heaven knows.
(But he might know nothing, said Greta.)
We talked about Living and Dying
until the food ran out . . .
It's hard to drift
like a gossamer veil
across a sky of Love
when you're fat, like me,
and anyway drink too much cappuccino.

I rode about in Mr Kraupl's
Bee-line taxi, reading magazines
and arranging my highlit hair.
Constantly think of how you look.
Walk tall and sit tall.
If you must think,
think calm and restful thoughts.
Keep yourself as firm
as your foundation garments.

You were far away,
trundling your wheel-barrow
full of goat-shit
in and out of the apple-trees.
The rain trickled over your knees
and into your big boots,
while the prayer-flags fluttered
in your Himalayan dreams.

Three days journey into Kashmir,
and you were still curled up
like a baby, refusing to look.
The drivers drove like maniacs
round and round the mountains
and when they reached Pamir
they shook hands
because it was over.
And what you wanted was pure air.

You arrived at 3 a.m.
and hugged me like a she-bear
with snow on its nose.
I ran about
in my little pointed shoes
looking for your *resting immobile Sat.*
I couldn't stop thinking
about my clothes; I said
We'll go to Norfolk where the sand
is full of gastropods like whelks
tunnelling into darkness
with their foot, or the sea-ear
who lives in pearl. How cool and nice!

While my daughter was doing a jigsaw
of The Quiet Bay,
we walked across the sandy turnip field
to the sea.

The sun was shining on the bungalows.
I felt as if a little pudding
were keeping warm inside me on a plate.
(*St John The Divine's life*
consisted in the pleasure
of shedding the possibilities
of pleasure, whispers Gee's
STEP-BY-STEP TO KNOWLEDGE
Encyclopaedia.)

Bid for the Summit

I thought of Schneider
and Aschenbrenner
who had been up here
nineteen years before.
They were our heroes.
We called them Ironfingers.

I lay face-downwards
in the Bergschrund.
The sun was unbearably hot.
Far away on the Silbersattel
a tiny dot was moving – ,
Walter, going down to Camp VII.

There are times, believe me,
when it is no disgrace to weep.
I heard the crunch
of his ten-pointers in the snow
and the silverfoil of his Coca-tee
being torn back.

How much I wanted them
up here beside me –
Walter and Otto and Hans –

walking towards me
with their arms outstretched
whispering Hermann, Hermann!

A Ski-ing Accident

Even the humble mole
dreams while he sleeps,
a little man as clean as a tomato.
Lives in hills, dreaming of a beetle coming in.

The presidents
dream of the presidents,
breaking their hearts on the piste.
Pineapple Lip Balm. Blood on her mitts.

Root Treatment

Three girls are sitting in a row.
They don't want to be here either.
One of them keeps fiddling with her shoe.

When I was in 'a mood',
my sister used to say
Leave her alone, Mother, leave her alone . . .

I'm lying on a boulder with an ant.
He is my sole companion.
He's running to the corner

with a hole in his hands.
It's warmer here
than in the waiting-room.

I used to be somebody's daughter.
I used to be so sweet.
She needs a good cry, said the matron,

she needs a good old cry . . .
Don't worry about your clothes, they said.
Don't worry about the blood-stains on your bib.

Members of the family
are crawling on my skin. They scratch
like beetles, but they can't come in.

All I can see is the nurse's face.
The nurse's face is miles away.
In Africa it must be very hot today.

If I move, I'll trip. What's that you say?
The dentist will remove
the blackberry pip.

He spreads the operating-table
with a sea of pads.
Good-bye, three girls, I'm going under.

Darling, take no notice
of the sea-gull
standing on your head.

To tell you the truth, I'm a doctor.
I'm not dressed in my coat, I know,
but I am going to kill you.

Leave them alone, Mother,
leave them alone . . . Look,
one of them is sitting in her shoe.

The Sea-Shore House

The sound of waves
comes creeping through the house
to stroke the sullen waters
of the garden, and my body,

like a stone, beside the garden,
begging, begging to be left untouched,
because she's bruising me:
may all her slow attempts
at getting close to me
fly off into the sound of waves
like birds with rock-grey wings!
I lie as still as someone
balancing a bowl of fruit
or rabbits on their head.

Beside the pond my dog
is gnawing bones
that crawl with ants,
and every now and then he stops
to rub his lips and nose
along the grass
that closes over him.
This afternoon aches
like a bell,
the sea is slow,
and if you come and look for me
beside the pool of melted water
you will find a stone
as cold and passionless as silk.

Silk is the liquid stone
my mother wore,
I see it slipping, slipping, like a skin;
I wear a scarf myself sometimes, I know,
to hide the scar
my mother made
I do not want to show:
my mother is afraid of love
and I, her silver-skinned
burnt only daughter –
tissue-head, peculiar, queen of pain –

I cry for kisses like she cries for shame.
The sound of waves
comes creeping through the house.

Early Nights

When people asked her
what her secret was,
she always answered
Early Nights.

She came upstairs
before I was asleep myself
sometimes, wearing a pair
of blue silk pyjamas.

I couldn't get to sleep
because the thought of silkworms
making silk in little boxes
gave me nightmares.

We had a magic word –
Przewalski
Przewalski –
to make them go away.

Przewalski was a captain
who was mad about Mongolia,
and trained wild horses
to 'die' for him.

Darling,
she used to say,
if praying doesn't work,
imagine visiting the zoo:

feel the lovely elephant,
the antelope, the gnu.
They sleep by the canal.
Recite their names.

It never works.
The captain
is a cruel man,
and I can't pronounce his name.

Geraniums

i
The yellow haddock
sinks into its milk.

The Giant Schnauzer
never stops running.

The Wagon Wheel
will soon be in my hand.

ii
Your dumb
familiar smell
of menstruation
fills the night air
like geraniums
where all your flying daughters

who like aloes
blossom only once
approach you:
can you see us
taxi-ing towards you
down the lights?

iii

She lives on Malibu and milk.
We had to carry her.
. . . her little stripey trousers . . .
Please come home

No one is sitting
in the chair of chairs
beside the pink geraniums tonight.
Her room-mates are

soft flabby puppies with large heads
in wedding shoes.
Their milky deaths
have only just begun.

iv

Mashed strawberries.
The slippery soap.
My mother's gone –
hurray, hurray, hurray!
The hotel has no bedroom, Madame.

I press myself
to silted ports
against the fish-tank's patient side.
Ejaculate, my pretty boy –
I'm dressed as an angel, Gabriel.

v

The sheets of the Hotel Royale
drying in the sun.
Cream. Bandages.
I never told him why.

vi

There is a little hole
in the universe

where light comes in
of a particular blue,

to bathe the clockwork
penguins on the floor

who are advancing
flipper tin tin tin

vii
The world's so soft
the pebbles on the beach
are like warm uteri.
I thought you would never come.

viii
I spend all day
among the fir-cones
and the hares
warming my bush.

A naked newt-collector
does not need to have a lover.
Rest your olive mouth
against my ear, I pray.

My bird is ginger-ruby,
court of flies.
Perhaps I should say now
I hate your kisses.

ix
. . . impressions of soft knives on ivory . . .
. . . tomato juice . . .
she doesn't even know
what he is doing.

x
Crack babies
crying all night in the hospital.

'Pelvic congestion.'
I need relief.

He brings a tray of tea
and little biscuits.
Sorry?
I thought you would never come.

xi
Look, we are leaving our husbands.
The garden is suddenly full

of people in long nighties
waving goodbye . . .

(You asked about suffering.
We feel guilty about Mama, I said.)

xii
I am a mother
living with sea-birds,

arranging yellow carols
on a plate.

O Comforter, draw near,
I make you Brownies:

feel my compassion
cut like steel.

xiii
Internal bleeding.
Pale blue.
She's only a baby.
I thought you would never come.

xiv
He feels for his penis
in the dark:

the smell of blood,
the smell of pink geraniums –

he's pulling Mummy's girls
across the park.

A Girl Called Owen

I was a disappointment,
not a boy:
they couldn't call me
Owen after all –
the brilliant young man
I should have been.

My father, who loved no one,
did love him:
bald as a pearl,
unlovable;
a naked sailor
in a world of bells.

*

Ah, just the two of us,
tilleuls, tilleuls.

He liked bare feet.
His wife died in great pain.

*

He was a little man
obsessed with light.

The sea was red
like peonies or glass.

He had a funny feeling in his
chest.

*

He made himself
a wooden hermitage
and sat on the verandah
drinking milk.

The moon was like a stone
he crushed with love.
The mountain-tops addressed
le rossignol.

His only friend
was buying sugared violets.
He didn't tell his son
that he was dying.

*

His son became a monk.
He saved the world.
I am the daughter
of his only friend.
They couldn't call me
Owen. I'm a girl.

*

Who am I?
I'm a rat.
I live downstairs.
Daylight
is an eyrie.
Give me wings.

Men

They walked in single file
along the paths
that were the only roads,
the men with eyes

like crunchy bones
I used to boil
when I was young,
and bleach out in the sun.

We fried fresh eggs
on flat stone walls,
and ate them with a spoon,
and then made love.

And now I feel
the sparrows' bones
filling my mouth
like blood-pink foam,

pink as the gentle dog-rose
that the men call home.

The Unsuccessful Wedding-Night

It's all because of Buster.
Of course, it's unreasonable,
he couldn't possibly have come –
his barking, his midnight walk,
the way he scratches at the blankets –

but as she presses her face
into the pillow of the small hotel,
she can't help missing him
terribly. She imagines the two of them
hiking in bright sunshine

over the Western Ghats; and soon
she begins to whimper to herself,
her runny nose trailing
over the foam pillows
like the Vasco da Gama of snails.

Crepúsculo – Ibiza

And he was famous
for the way he handled girls.
He was like a butcher with a knife.
I followed him.

My little knock –
so high-pitched, so final.
Remembering what?
Somebody saying Of course,
if it's your first gala,
you will be nervous.

He smiled, and singed my hair
with his gold-plated
cigarette-lighter.

The doctor came too late.
It was snowing.
He put a box of chocolates
on my bed, and kissed my cheek.
You're a good girl, he said.

His long white skirts,
his polished shoes,
his soft pink hands
that never touched my lips.

He sent me photographs
of naked men
on diving boards
and decks of yachts.
Crepúsculo – Ibiza.
Shell Bay. Torquay.
La carte postale de l'amitié.
Jean Genet's Liverpool.

We used to do this
in the war, he said,

marching all night in our sleep,
then hiding in a bluebell wood,
crying out loud for girls.

He carries apples in his coat.
His mother thinks he's dying.
He hears white cows that move about
when he's alone at night.

The Ptarmigan Hunter

i

I'm being kept awake
by too many kisses

and the new central-heating system
of a high-rise Carousel hotel.

The hot pipes go *tick tick*
and this man I hardly know

keeps turning me over and over
like the hunter on the radio

who came across a mummy
while on holiday in Greenland.

ii

Lady of Qilakitsoq,
sleeping on ice,

your face tattooed
by the old woman

with the seal-bone needle,
your body wrapped

in cormorant skins
and polar willow leaves,

sleep
while you can . . .

iii
An off-duty ranger
drove over in his Dodge from Umanak

to shoot ptarmigan,
and found a young woman, freeze-dried,

like coffee, under a rock.
He cut off her black underclothes

and took them home to his father
who, being afraid of ghosts,

fed them into the Garbage Guzzler
he had just bought.

The Bath

He presses an oval of soap
into the palm of his hand
and twirls the bristles in the violet foam

until it quilts his fingers like the snow
where trappers crawl to pull the hairs
from little Russian weasels.

I lie under the greying water; drape
my flannel on my curls
like palls, or like the coloured coats

that poodles wear; or muslin
lain on cheese in dingy larders
to protect it from the flies.

Not that he's likely to look:
his only joy's his — twizzle twizzle twizzle —
obsessive pirouettes. Then I remember

He's been dead for weeks.
I roll over in the water thoughtfully,
feeling – not lonely exactly –

more like a floating pear-half
having warm chocolate sauce poured over me.

Umbrella Man

Enclose me, auburn fly-keeper, like them
in your warm-blooded hands that comfort me.

The flies, ordained, impaled, neat, display
their silver hips for your consideration;

their soft, picked, feather wings embrace
the summer air. You eat blue plums; you fish;

you trick the underwater world with flies
as beautiful, as lost as me. Surround me.

Eating Chocolates in the Dark

And after that, the diaries stop.
We think he went to his grandmother's,
whom he adored apparently.
They sat on her bed
with the lights turned off,
and ate chocolates,
and listened to the sea.
It was a kind of ritual
they both found very comforting.

Her other love was hyacinths.
He said he didn't like them,
and asked her to take them away.

And then he started telling her
about a lost eskimo
who paddled up the Don in a kayak.
He was dressed in sealskin,
and very tired. After a few days,
he caught a cold and died.

The dip dip dip of the little boat,
and his sad story-telling voice,
were like a lullaby,
and she was asleep, or nearly asleep,
when suddenly he asked her
if she believed in God.
(She told me all this quite openly –
the old Russian grandmother,
half lying back on her cushions.

Perhaps I shouldn't say this, she said,
but listen to me for a moment –
if you wake up,
and feel something fat like a puppy
wriggling between your legs,
you're not going to say it's God,
or the answer to all your questions,
or Love, are you? It's sex!
It was the same for him.)

The Last Flight of the Friendship 27

Please don't hold me
as if I was an armful of carnations
about to fall apart –

with a *pink pink pink*
as far as Casablanca
and the end of time –

pink sand, pink sunset,
and our Friendship 27's
high-pitched pinking

décollage . . .
It only makes it worse, your saying
It sounds like a chaffinch!

Primulas

I walked three miles
to buy your dog a lead.

Now walk into the park
beside the sea.

The primulas
look sickly in the dark.

The gardeners are asleep
beside their wives.

The wheel-barrows sleep
in painted sheds.

He's NOT allowed to sleep
on people's beds!

Fo-toy. The french for comfort.
Do sit down.

Lie back against his fur
and dream of me.

My nightie rides up
somewhere round my chin.

So please don't look.
My body's very thin.

I walked three miles
to buy your dog a lead.

Saying Goodbye to the Suzuki Man

Like my father's last orange,
I thought this kiss
would be the sweetest one –

he left the curls of peel
by his bed for me to find
when I found the body:

Ssss in bright orange.
From you, I have nothing,
not even a *beep beep beep*.

Mother Stone

My father was a tall man who approved of beating,
but my mother, like a mother stone,
preferred us to be sitting in a small room
lined with damson-coloured velvet
thinking quietly to ourselves, undisturbed;
everything was slow and beautiful
when we were being punished: all we had to do
was watch the dark-red petals' roses
press against each other in a slight breeze
on the window pane, and blossoms fall
in silence from the cherry-tree;

and now my son is lying in a long white shirt
across our eiderdown, trying to stay awake,
and fingering my spine's shell pink as if I were a beach
and he were blades of marram grass in drifts of sand.

I dab my face with cream that smells of cucumber
and whisper in a distant milky voice
Of course I'll wake you up when he comes;
and then his eyelids close,
and in his self-created darkness he is following
a big car on a motorway at night,
it turns into the driveway to the house,
and presently the driver gets out:
it is only a bear in the moonlight,
walking on the lavender beds.

No one

No one is to touch me
but the Lord.

His finger-tips caress me
like a knife.

Everywhere I go
I am adored.

I want to be a monk
but I'm a wife.

Not all the women of England

At the top of the bank
a blonde airman
is doing sit-ups
in the tenderest
of early-morning sun.
I want to squash him flat.
He's like my Uncle Pat's
gold cigarette-case

that flies open
when you touch it.

You cruise along the fence
with your elbow
on the rolled-down window-edge.
*Everything you come near
falls to bits.*

The cattery sells bedding-plants
and runner-beans.
Someone has been up here
to mow a tiny lawn,
and hang a sign above it,
opposite the fence I mentioned
and the bank, before the airman came.

The way the green brim
of your Chinese sun-hat's
been turned up –
it's like the tail
on a bulldog's bum.
Help me to take no notice,
holy flowers!

The passenger, the passenger,
I don't want to be the passenger.
Please can we stop at the Trout Lakes.

You came into my bedroom
carrying a duck,
for we lived together happily
for five years.
(She was so tame,
they wrote about her
in the *Whitby Gazette*.)
And now you're driving a saloon
I've come to hate

round and round the camp
like a bum.
I think I'm going to say
I want to leave you.
I want to leave you.

The hearts on the shutters
make the houses look like
cuckoo-clocks, or little chalets –
can you hear the cow-bells tinkle? –
where Mother Bear and Father Bear
eat fondue. They overlook
the fence and the bank.

The airman walks away
to living-quarters
we can't see
like a zoo animal.
He polishes his boots.
He's far from home.
Deep in trout lakes on the other side
trouts' dreams of flies
come true . . .

Not all the women of England
are boiling kettles
by the tall gates
but I love them all.
They shelter in the oaks
on the soft verges
where the airman lights up
his king-size cigarette.

The Assumption

I am lying by an upstairs window
like a horse.
My mane is beautiful.
I am a huge balloon.
My legs are swelling.
till they push me to my feet.
Now I can trot to the window.

Fat air is pulling me
beyond the lacy curtains,
they get in my mouth
like peach-skin.
The children are calling
in a little piping ring
like fledglings.

Help me – my legs are wet,
and my broad wings
are taking me away.
And you, Rosanne, squatting
in the sun with your flippers on:
Wave! It's too late to stop me now.
I can see acres of turquoise,

surrounded by acres of men.
They are the objects of my desire.
My eyes harden their bodies,
and hood their regal eyes.
My hooves kick out their hearts,
and make them beat like mine,
my wing-beats make shamans of them.

The flies are so thick
at the pool-side
they have to part them like nets,
when the muscular girl

who's my best friend
plunges in at the deep-end
and swims far out to sea.

Ouarzazate

Flies are entering
my mouth.
They drink
at my eyes.
They love them.

I've lost my hands
so how can I
brush them away?
*C'est toujours midi,
Madame.*

My heart goes
boom pause boom pause boom.
Don't touch me,
je vous en prie,
or I'll kill you.

The Coronation
of the Long-Distance Walker

I am the queen of daisies.
I deal in rabbits and bees.

I have been to Africa
where stones pile up

like parcels
for Latifa, Fatima,

girls who are good.
Here there are dog-leads,

moments of hope:
when the tide is low,

see Murasaki, golden lady,
far out on my father's bed.

Jacko's Girl

Send me a real dog-faced ape
that rides a dog, and plays the harp
or lute, who goes 'la la la la'
and stands up upside-down in the park.

We'll walk round flower-beds,
through rooms of light,
looking for the room I fell in love in,
singing *Stella Maris* in my bra.

That's where the velvet monkey lived.
I wanted him. I saw his dark red fingers
crush his dress.
He was my sister Mary's doll, not mine.

My present was my first geranium,
that smelled of peppermints and had no bones.
It was a post. I wanted a baboon.
They come from Abyssinia in crates.

Visiting the Zoo

The tall giraffes can never sit.
Their names are Valerie and Gwendoline.

I am their tall reticulated son.
This is our sand and hay.

Follow our gold strip to holy Tassili,
blonde swallow-tails, hares, a little milk.

You are a good girl. He will never know
you are in love with someone else, not him.

The Small-Mammal House

My twin sister Mary leans against a cage
where little kinkajous are watching her with interest.

Arboreal nocturnal sort of bears
with a passion for your chocolate, I see.

All I got was bits of chewing-gum –
your 'sapodilla-gum-tree-juice-gum', chickle.

Who took the photo anyway?
You shouldn't let them when you look like that.

'*Glissez, mortels, n'appuyez-pas*, GLISSEZ!'
Remember Louli, with her ear-muff hair?

'Tippy-toes, tippy-toes, tall as you can!
Reach up to those forbidden chocolates, Mary!'

You were my elective mute, becoming almost elegant
in time to Louli's elevating music . . .

It isn't good to watch small mammals by the hour,
all hunched-up. Also, funny men go down there, Mummy
                                                said.

The Monkey Boys

Panare boys, Panare boys,
running through the jungle with blow-pipes
to shoot capuchin, you don't like the creoles
with their long white cocks one bit:
when they see your necklaces
of capybara teeth and black nut shells,
they laugh.

Their wandering cows
have eaten all the salt you saved
to sprinkle on ten roasting peccaries
and shrimp for boys who will be men tomorrow . . .
And when they see your feathered bandoliers
and deer-hoof charms,
they laugh and laugh;

and they don't care
if there's no salt
swinging from the bow-wood tree
in Campa, Chanchamayo, by the silver river;
and anyway you will be dead,
your bodies wrapped
in green cane beds, tomorrow.

Parrots

I am surrounded by parrots.
They leave their chopped tomatoes on my head.
They pile at my feet like dying socks.

Their lettuce-coloured shoulders are so heavenly
the people at the zoo go mad about them.
One of them is looking in my eyes,

and saying, *What's the matter, Billy?* (meaning me).
Catch them, someone, take them back to Paradise,
they're giving me a terrible disease.

Topsy

Topsy, not you, 's my guardian angel now.
She leans against the Arizona air
like foxgloves and ignores me: I feel free.
Her lips say *Take no notice* to the sand.

You, on the other hand, doze in your chair
all day, then hop about the bed all night
as if your jealousy
was eczema. What a fuss!

Topsy lives on wild grapes and thistles,
moving slowly, almost pink; tired
of subduing Indians along the border;
calm as milk.

My children cover me with wings
like moths or hoods,
I can't see where I'm going.
It's not fair.

Hackberries hang in the moonlight,
Topsy thinks.
Topsy thinks
The desert smells of rain.

At the end of the [American] Civil War, when the government was no longer able to care for the camels, they were dispersed: some were sold to circuses, some as transport animals in Mexico, some to a mine in Nevada; while others were freed in Arizona, where their progeny roamed wild until at least 1905. The last survivor of this herd was a female named Topsy who was captured in the Arizona Desert and sent to the Los Angeles Zoo, where she died in 1934.

From *The Camel: Its Evolution, Ecology, Behavior and Relationship to Man* by Hilde Gauthier-Pilters and Anne Innis Dagg – University of Chicago Press, 1981.

Looking for Camels

She followed him all afternoon,
although he didn't speak to her,
or even turn to watch her
climb the dusty road.
White moths settled on her feet.
She saw a mule
with ants inside its ear.
M'sieur, m'sieur, the children cried,
running through poppies
with silver knives . . . Boar droppings.
Snake country . . . *Of course I know*
exactly where we are.

He walked into the mountains
like a man who's on his way
to kill a dog. He didn't stop.
She closed her eyes to let a drop
of calamine run down her cheek.
Somewhere sandy, somewhere soft,
that's what he had promised her . . .
She wrote a letter home in her head:
There's nothing here but rock,
she began,
and his Hi-Tec Hi-Tec Hi-Tec
footsteps in the snow.

Devotion

i

My darling camel,
I want to tell you very clearly
I feel normal.
All those years of coming here
in black with P. are over.
Say you're interested.
You're so disdainful!

ii

Phlegmatic, waterless, you trot,
but sometimes pace, like bears.
Deaf goats and hens
climb up and down your neck.
We ship and slaughter you.
We drink your blood.

iii

I spent the days in boxes
keeping quiet.
The blue fish on the cushions
were my friends.
And during all that time
I didn't come.

iv

And then one day, my darling,
I was your *freshly-washed injected devotee*.
I stood beside your moat
with my nurse.

v

Please kiss me with your flaccid lips.
Roam free. Sweet waters of the dayas, rise.
Your feet are like an ostrich's.

You carry gold in goat-skin water-bags.
You carry brides.

vi

At sunset, I go home with the zoo-man.
His hands are like enormous teddy-bears.

The Culmination
Of All Her Secret Longings

Write to her, by all means,
but remember,
she can't concentrate
like she used to.
And don't expect her
to write back.

We all miss you so much
as you can imagine.
Signs of mice at Greenfields
but not too bad.
Lots of lovely little lambs.
There was one in Betty's yard,
and she caught it
for Christobel to stroke.

What's that you say?
Your plastic gloves have split?
Just make a little opening
in the zip.

Dear Laura,
We both thought your room was very nice.
It's lovely to have clean clothes
and surfaces, etc. The coalman's been.

Could you make friends with Rory?
He seemed such a nice boy.

Of course she's dotty.
You put an orange on the table
and she's frightened of it.
Oh no, she's never been like this before.
All one can do is keep her nighties clean,
and all her things.
She wants a book on the Sahara now.
And she's not supposed to read.

'Camels deprived of salt
may eat their own fur
or that of other camels.'

And she's not supposed to read at all, you know.
She came into the day-room and tipped the Scrabble
all over the floor –
believe me, it's a mad-house in there!

'A captive female
that was ignored by a male
cried out, rolled on the floor,
urinated at frequent intervals,
pawed the ground,
jumped, kicked,
and lay down repeatedly,
merely on hearing the call
of a male she could not see.'

I wake up at midday
and loneliness, in pink,
gets down on her knees to pray.
Relax, I hear him say, *my dear, relax*.

Bobby has been staying here,
and has been smitten by the same desire as me,
i.e., to buy a pair of Lederhosen!

Naked but for our Lederhosen
and a glazing of Ambre Solaire!
Don't say I didn't warn you!

'. . . an insect, a lizard track, a prehistoric tool . . .'

Betty says to tell you
she can't go on for ever!
Am thinking of you v. much.
Nothing awful's happened,
I hope. Dr K was just a sod.
The other one was just a boy
who looked so ill
I thought he was going to be sick.
I felt so sorry for him.
I quite forgot to leave the box of dates.
Love, Babs.

'The Tuareg poisoned
the members of the Flatters Expedition
by mixing oleander with their dates.
Man is said to die
who eats small crickets
that have eaten it.'

Patience, patience.
You were next on the list anyway.
We have called her Sandy.
I felt the midwife should've thanked *me*
for providing *her*
with such a gentle and pleasant experience!

'It made a humming noise
as it was eased from the vulva
by the herder pulling on its legs.'

I want to give them all
a lovely evening!

'Abrading their teeth
with charcoal and bones
and occasional mummified young gazelle.'

Remember the sand-dunes,
each more lovely than the last,
and the oranges . . .
Perhaps I shouldn't say this, my dear,
but there's a part of me
that wants to be there with you.
Chris is crying.
I had better go.

Dear Rory,
When Laura's lying down,
you'll see a shaved door.
Open the little door,
and shake the batteries out.
They'll all come tumbling out onto the floor.
This will be the best thing for all of us.
And please tell the nurse
to keep her pink flap clean.

'During the rut his swollen testicles
increased greatly in weight.'

Please understand
I had no hand in this.
It was ENTIRELY B's idea.
(Mother has always forgotten me,
ever since I was born.)
P.S. The stuff was *Floramel*,
or *Fluormel*, I think.

'. . . lures of dried shark and sardines . . .
. . . succulent parakelia near Alice Springs . . .'

Have I ever told you
that when I was at school

I was absolutely CONVINCED
we were all in a mental home,
and only *I* knew the secret,
and the teachers-stroke-nurses
were secretly rather afraid of me?

Thus starry but carry,
woollen but coolly,
local but velocity,
muddy but muddle.

Do you want any food?
I could send a parcel
of chocs or something.
Betty's away.
Did you get the dictionary O.K.?

'. . . covering on camel and on foot
a distance far greater
than that between the earth and the moon . . .'

It's been delicious here,
the bluebells and the sweet grass,
and when I smell the little jar
of ointment by your bed I think
O Laura, come home soon.

'It is believed that this moisture
is stored in pores and fissures in the rock.
The last heavy rain fell
several thousand years ago.'

Dear Laura, I fell in love,
consummated the relationship,
and was jilted in favour of another man,
all in the space of five days.
P.S. The Desert is well worth a visit!

'. . . the desert where long sand-storms
make all projects vain . . .'

Bobby spent the WHOLE TIME
locked inside his room –
reading the *Financial Times*!
He says he can't stand being in the country!

'We collected at least 40 freshly-produced pellets,
and weighed them immediately in a cotton bag.'

O.K., but you must realise
everyone has a different way
of 'just being themselves'
which is frequently most annoying
to other people.

Be a good girl, Laura.
When you're better,
there'll be plenty of books at home,
and all your things.
Everyone has blood tests.
Dadda doesn't mind them a bit.

'Kenyan nomads
mix camel milk with blood.
They obtain the blood
from strong reclining camels
by shooting an arrow
at close range
into the jugular.
When 1–2 litres have been collected,
the wound is dressed with dung . . .'

Bobby has gone –
so you have missed the chance
of watching our subtle exchange
of loving, intimate glances –
probably just as well.
Keep writing. I love it.
But why does this person always leave you in tears?

'He utters the same blo-blo-blo sound,
protruding his dulaa
and rubbing his occiput
against his sinking shoulder.'

We are going to Morocco on the 6th
so stick it out until we get back anyway.
Obviously we can't ring from Agadir,
but we gave your number to Babs.

'Camelids are the only ungulates
that copulate in a couched position.'

Dear Laura, No more apologies!
Betty and I are thinking of you,
eating chicken thighs in bed with Rory,
both of you nearly asleep!
(Largactil gravy on your lips,
insult to the yearning soul . . .)
No news from Morocco,
but I expect they're you-know-what.

'He sits on her dusty back
so that his sternal callosity
rests on the rear of her hump.
His hind legs thus remain
completely folded.
He dribbles saliva and blows,
blows out his dulala.'

HAPPY BIRTHDAY LAURA!
We are trying to fix everything up
so you can come here soon.
Lots of rats and bob-cats. You'll love it!
Waiting for a bus to Goulimine!

'Unlike lamoids
female camels

spread their legs apart
and grunt.'

What a clever girl –
allowed out with Rory!
But O the corridors are long.
You won't come back again.
Is it true you like getting letters?
In which case, why don't the doctors send you some?
Or can't they write?

'Brides on camels in the Gulf Of Carpentaria
combating mange with an ointment of Stockholm tar.'

The letters give her iron nerves
and an uncrushable will.
Your tender words warm the soul,
she feels cleaner, uplifted.
Do not be shy of tender words, he told them.

'After copulation,
he falls away sideways,
before standing up to graze and sing.'

It took Th. Monod 8 days to walk through a monospecific pasture of *A. pungens* in the Majabat-al-Konbra. Rory, the psychiatric nurse, walked with him, and they were joined by a woman wearing a clean pair of pyjamas, followed by a healthy-looking camel. *My new address is Sand*, she was saying. *Write to me by all means*, she said.